Garnishing & Decorating

Creative Ideas with More than 330 Step-by-step Illustrations

4880 Lower Valley Road, Atglen, Pennsylvania 19310

Elisabeth
Bangert

Garnishing &
Decorating

Creative Ideas with More than
330 Step-by-step Illustrations

Contents

Hand Tools

■ Knives

For various kitchen work, special knives are necessary. If you would like to expand your personal assortment of knives for garnishing and decorating, you should make sure when buying them that the knives are forged of stainless hardened steel. It is not important whether the handle is made of wood or plastic, but it must fit well in your hand.

Chef's Knife (1)

For cutting large, hard fruits such as pineapple or watermelon, you would do best to use a chef's knife. It makes a clean cut through even the toughest fruits.

Medium Kitchen Knife (2)

A medium kitchen knife helps you with the somewhat coarser work, such as cutting up medium-sized fruits, sausage, or chunk cheese.

Small Paring Knife (3)

For fine work, especially for peeling, you need a small, handy kitchen knife. It must have a very sharp blade and a point, so that you can, for example, cut into sensitive fruits or remove their skins.

Waved Knife (4)

With the waved blade of this knife you can, for example, cut fruits and vegetables, butter and cheese decoratively into waved pieces.

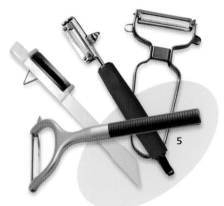

Sparing Parer (5)

As the name indicates, this peeler helps you to peel fruits and vegetables as sparingly as possible with little pressure. The more pressure you apply or the more steeply you hold the parer, the thicker the skin is removed. There are now the most varied peelers, which often include other handy tools, such as a zigzag cutter and a channeling knife. No matter whether the blade is longitudinal or transverse, all have the same function. Simply try them and see which fits best in your hand.

Vegetable Slicer or Mandoline (6)

To cut vegetables and fruits into fine slices it is best to use the vegetable slicer. Always put the slicer on a non-skid surface or on the rim of a bowl. Many slicers are equipped with a practical and, above all, safe finger guard. In good kitchen shops you will find slicers with ceramic blades. They are sharpened from both sides and suitable for dishwashers.

■ Work Surface

Without a practical work surface, the best cutting tool will not fulfill its purpose!

Glass Work Surface (1)
Glass has the advantage of being very hygienic, easy to clean and neutral in taste and smell. Glass surfaces are heat-resistant and machine-washable as a rule. Make sure there are skid-free feet.

Cutting Board (2)
You should also have cutting boards on hand. The foods to be prepared grip them well, and your knives will thank them for this cutting surface. The blades will not become dull so quickly! To cut juicy fruits or meat, you should have a cutting board with a juice channel.

Work Plate in the Kitchen (3)
If you have a kitchen with a covering plate of natural stone, you can consider yourself lucky. These surfaces are not only very heat-resistant, but also especially suitable for working with toppings, since they are essentially cold. For all further work, such as rolling out dough or shaping marzipan, it is important that the plate be free from bits of material and as smooth as possible. You might dust it with some flour, so that nothing sticks to it.

■ Cutter

To give foods, especially fruits and vegetables, a decorative outside, the most varied cutters can be had. Whether round, angled, or circular—appropriate aids for all imaginable shapes are available.

Ball and Pearl Cutter (1)
Whether ball- or pearl-shaped, there are cutters with metal heads in varied sizes. With these utensils you can cut out evenly round balls. Push the metal head deep into the fruit or vegetable, and cut the fruit pulp out by making a further turn.

Cookie Cutter (2)
Cutters made of metal or plastic have a great many uses. Whether fruit, vegetable, dough or marzipan—it is no real challenge for the cutters with the sharp edges. You can even cut sausage and cheese into unusual shapes with them. Depending on what you want to cut, you should make sure that the cutters are not too filigreed.

Cutter with Ejector (3)
If you want to make especially delicate decorations of, for example, blanched vegetables or marzipan, a cutter with an ejector helps. The ejector loosens the cutout piece from the cutter very lightly when you press a button.

Apple Corer (4)
A practical aid for cutting out the core of a whole apple.

Apple Slicer (5)
To divide an apple evenly into slices. In addition, the core is also cut out by it.

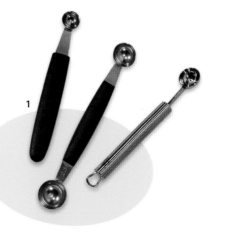

7

Egg Slicer (6)

Surely practical, but not absolutely necessary. With it you can cut hard-boiled eggs into thin slices (round or oval) and use them in the preparation of small pieces of egg.

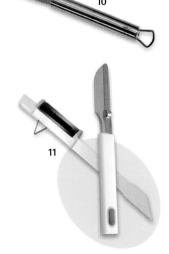

Spiral Cutter (7)

With it you can make large spirals of radishes or zucchini. Make especially sure that the vegetables to be cut are fresh. Woody radishes, for one, are very hard to work with this tool.

Butter Cutter (8)

With this tool you can cut the otherwise monotonous butter into the most varied shapes, with wavy lines, as balls or rolls.

Butter Shaper (9)

Another practical aid for garnishing with butter. It can not only be used to shape butter, but is also extremely suited for, as example, cutting out the pulp of squash.

Channeling Knife (10)

With this knife you can cut spirals out of the rind of citrus fruits, that will, for example, turn every cocktail into a highlight. You can
also cut off the rind of a cucumber in strips.

Zigzag Cutter (11)

With it you can, above all, cut large fruits and vegetables in zigzag form along a line. Then turn the fruit or vegetable halves carefully against each other and pull them out.

Classy Cutter (12)

The world's fastest zigzag cutter cuts the interiors of fruits, eggs, etc., into zigzag forms. The objects to be cut are placed in the cutter. Simply by turning the plastic housing, you turn the knives through the fruits and they are completely cut through.

Zester (13)

With its five small blades, you scratch the rind from oranges or lemons. Thus you obtain orange or lemon zest quickly and simply for decorating, cooking, and baking.

Potato Spiral (14)

Even potatoes can be made into decorative elements: Simply screw the potato spiral into the long axis until the round cutting knife becomes visible at the other end. Then, with light pressure from above on the cutout spiral, turn the cutting knife backward. Thus you will pull the potato spiral out with it.

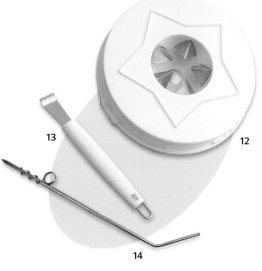

There are some practical kitchen appliances that can help you in your garnishing work and make the results even better. About these devices one can simply say: "Nice to have!"

Lemon Squeezer (1)

Whether it is made of metal or plastic is merely a question of esthetics. It is important, though, that the squeezer has a bowl to catch the juice. The fruits were cut in half, the halves set onto the squeezer and turned under pressure to squeeze out the juice. If you first roll the lemon on the table, you then get more juice out of it. You often need lemon juice for garnishing and decorating. Thus the squeezer is a really useful aid.

Blender (2)

A powerful multi-mixer spins and reduces everything quickly and thoroughly. With it you can mix tropical fruits into fruit cocktails or puree them for desserts. Thus you develop tastes that no single fruit satisfies!

Food Processer (3)

Essentially, a hand mixer is fully sufficient. In most cases, though, you get better results from this machine, especially when beating cream, butter crème or sand-cake dough. Through the mixing technology, the material becomes much foamier and looser.

1

3

2

■ Garnishing Tools

For baking, garnishing of cakes or squeezing out frostings, very special tools are needed.

Kitchen Brush (1)
To spread egg on baked goods or coat them with glaze. Practical for this are, above all, are
the new silicon brushes.

Piping Bag (4)
Not only cream and butter crème, but also various fresh cheese preparations and soft butter, can be given a decorative form with this tool. It is important to clean the bag thoroughly after every use. Don't fill the bag too full, and make sure that no air enters it, if possible.

Nozzle (5)
Various nozzles allow very different patterns to be made. The round nozzle creates a smooth, round shape for points or lines, while the star nozzle forms rosettes and the flat nozzle creates wide stripes.

Spatula (2)
Without it, neat coating of a cake with cream or crème is not possible. With a little practice, you will surely have a lot of fun with it.

Garnishing Comb (3)
With it you can create fantastic effects, such as on the edges of a cake. Simply press the comb on flat and pull it along the edge without lifting it.

Piping Cone

To make, for example, filigreed ornaments, a piping bag is necessary. You can make them quickly yourself with little effort or material:

1. Cut a piece of parchment or baking paper from the roll and divide it diagonally.

2. Role one triangle from the thin side into a small cone.

3. Fill the cone with covering material.

4. Fold the cone together from the wide end until the paper applies light pressure to the interior. Then cut off the tip with scissors according to the desired thickness of the ornament.

The Right Utensils for a Buffet

Whoever plans a buffet for friends or relatives should consider the following questions from the start: "Where will the buffet be set up?" and "What utensils do I need for it?"

Basically it is very simple: Whoever has lots of space puts a table in the center of the room, so that one can walk around it. Then everything goes off smoothly in turn. Whoever has less space puts the table at the wall and determines the order of approach.

Naturally, nice platters are also needed for optical success. But who has that many "silver platters?"

You can do it very simply: The one heirloom, the nice silver platter, simply gets put in the middle of the buffet. Alas, some foods cannot be placed in direct contact with silver. Eggs, for example, color the silver black, and the taste of such things as fish and eggs changes. For this reason, silver and other metal platters are usually coated thinly with aspic. In this way too, the platters are not scratched when foods are taken from them. But caution: Don't put fresh pineapple or kiwi on the aspic, or it will soften!

White dinner plates of somewhat larger cutting boards, which are made of white plastic or glass nowadays, are suitable, as are round metal serving platters that can be turned easily. If platters have become unsightly with age, one can wrap them in aluminum foil. It is important, though, that the materials will not affect foods. Appropriately sized plates should be available three times for every guest, or a plate should be on hand for every offered course.

Baskets of all kinds are suitable for bread, rolls, and fruit. Simple glass bowls with no ornamentation look best for salads. The foods should make the impression, not the utensils.

Along with the eating utensils, which as a rule should be on hand three times for every guest, suitable serving utensils are also needed. Salad forks, gravy spoons, and meat forks should be correctly placed. A fork and a spoon can be ready for each plate, and on two ends of large platters. Do not skimp with the serving utensils, or else you will have to count on the guests serving themselves with their own utensils.

Plenty of glasses should be on hand for all the drinks.

Squeezed Garnishings

First attach the desired nozzle to the piping bag and fill the bag half-full of the crème or cream. Close it at the end by twisting it. Hold the bag in your left hand and lightly press the closing with your right hand.

1. **Rosette:** Turn the bag with the nozzle once in a circle and pull the nozzle away while turning it slightly. Or if you would like it fancier:

2. **Rosette:** Move the bag with the star nozzle twice in a circle and pull the nozzle away while turning it slightly. Rosettes go very nicely with fruits or chocolate beans.

3. **Star:** Hold the bag with the star nozzle upright and spray on one point. When it reaches the desired size, pull the nozzle away upward.

4. **Ornaments:** Move the bag with the round nozzle in even motions.

5. **Ribbon:** Individual points close together make a nice ribbon, which can be used, for example, along the rim of a cake. This can also be done with stars or rosettes.

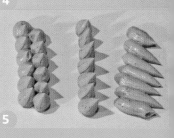

The Foods

When you shop for groceries to be garnished or decorated, quality and freshness matter most, especially for fruits, vegetables, milk products, eggs, meat, and cold cuts. You can get them most reliably from your "family grocery store" where they know you and can also give you reliable advice. At home, you should store the foods as quickly as possible into the refrigerator, freezer, food drawer, or cellar. When you then start to make garnishes, all the foods that you will use that are in the refrigerator should be left there for as long as possible. Thus their decorations will keep their fresh appearance and taste to the end.

■ Fruits

For garnishing with fruit, you should always make sure to use unhandled fruits. Often you must work with the rinds of the fruits and thus avoid giving yourself and your guests unnecessary poisons. When you buy fruit, also make sure that you get the right degree of ripeness—ripe, but not overripe. When you work with fruits for garnishing

and they do not contain enough of their own fruit acids, it is recommended to sprinkle them with lemon juice at once. Thus with apples, pears, avocados, etc., you can avoid their turning brown from the effect of oxygen. This problem is especially great with bananas. To be able to work with them in garnishing, you must dip them in lemon juice regularly, so they do not turn black. And their flavor also suffers in the process. Thus they are not very suitable for garnishing.

■ Vegetables

For vegetables, too, the degree of ripeness is decisive. In addition, with tomatoes, cucumbers, etc., one must not forget always to season them well. They do not have such an intensive flavor as fruits.

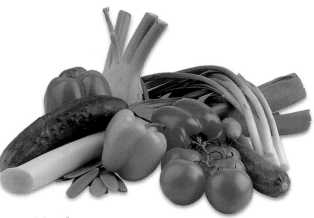

■ Herbs

Fresh herbs give the garnish that certain zing; they are the dot on the **i** of their "creation." Dried herbs do not have this effect. They do not look nearly as attractive on the platter, nor do they provide their full flavor any more, or contain as many vitamins.

■ Fresh Dairy Products

With butter, cream, cheese, etc., the freshness is naturally most important. When you work with butter for garnishing, it is thus advisable to have a small pan of ice water at hand, so you can always keep the butter pieces cold. On the table or buffet you should also work with this method and serve butter on ice. Thus your butter decorations will not only look good longer, but also keep their flavor longer.

Sweet Garnishes

When using chocolate, marzipan, and glazes, always choose products of the best quality. When working the sweet morsels, you will then find that it paid not to scrimp here.

Fish

Along with the absolute freshness of fish products, their appearance is also an important point that you should not underestimate in all garnishes for fish. Consider precisely for what occasion you want to put your fish creations on the table or buffet and whom you have invited as guests. Always remember that not everyone wants to look a fish in the eye while eating it!

Meat

When you garnish meat products, keep in mind that the meat should be cooked only briefly and never cooked to death. The meat will dry out more when it stands on the buffet platter a long time, and it will very soon taste old.

A Word in Closing

Please be careful to use as little inedible material as possible for garnishes. Sometimes, as in the case of toothpicks for canapés or cheese-melon spears, this cannot be avoided and is also a practical aid for eating. String, paper, and bows, though, have no place on plates and platters.

A Few Tips for Garnishing & Decorations

The good old bit of kitchen wisdom, "The eye eats along with you," sounds somewhat old-fashioned to many nowadays. But this does not change the fact that, even today, it has lost none of its validity. There is nothing more appetizing than an optically inspiring plate or a lovingly decorated buffet. Garnishes like those that we show you in this book thus will surely add much to the relaxed atmosphere and the satisfaction of your guests.

But do not go too far, for here too it is true that less is more! An overloaded platter, on which one can no longer recognize the foods under the garnishes, is more likely to scare the guest away, as he won't want to disturb the artistic creations.

Please always consider that the prepared foods and garnishes will be eaten, Nobody likes to eat what has passed through many fingers or no longer looks like something edible.

Also make sure to keep an eye on your arrangements at all times. Unappetizing platters with leftovers should be removed and arranged anew in the kitchen.

Apples

Ingredients for 2 Apple Fans
½ Apple (such as Granny Smith)
Lemon juice for sprinkling

Garnishing Tool:
Paring knife

Apples are especially thankful fruits. One often has them on hand at home, and an effective decoration can be conjured up with them quickly and inexpensively at any time of the year. It is important that the pulp of the apple is still firm. The decorations are especially nice when the skin color is even. With two different colors, striking effects can be achieved.

Decorative Apple Fans

1. Quarter the apple half. Do not remove the core, just even it a bit so the quarter can stand on it.

2. Set the apple quarter on the core. Put the kitchen knife in at an angle .1 inches from the edge and cut out a V-shaped piece.

3. In the same way, cut out five or six more pieces, until you reach the middle of the piece of apple.

4. To finish, connect the V-shaped pieces somewhat offset to make a quarter.

Tip:

The Granny Smith with its firm pulp makes a striking figure with its even, fresh green color.

Ingredients for one Swan:
½ Apple (such as Red Delicious)
Lemon juice for sprinkling

Garnishing Tools:
Paring knife
Toothpicks

Apple Swan

1. Cut the apple half into quarters. Even the core a bit, so the quarter can stand on it.

2. Set the quarter on the core and apply the knife at an angle .1 inches from the edge. Now cut out a V-shaped piece.

3. In the same way, cut out five or six more pieces until you reach the middle of the piece of apple.

4. For the swan's head, halve and peel another quarter of the apple. Now use the toothpick to carve the contours of the head and neck. Carefully cut out the swan's head with the knife along the contours.

5. To give the swan's head a firmer hold, cut a small notch out of the apple body.

Tip:

In any case, the apple swan is a real eye-catcher and makes as good a figure on a nice cheese or cold-cuts platter as on a dessert. Firm red apples, such as Red Delicious or Braeburn, are suitable.

Ingredients for one Blossom:
1-2 Apples (such as Braeburn)
.7 ounces Pistachio nuts (whole and chopped)
Lemon juice for sprinkling

Garnishing Tool:
Paring knife

Apple Blossom

1. Quarter the apple. Do not remove the core; just cut it fairly flat with the paring knife.

2. Cut out a triangular piece at each of the two narrow ends of the apple.

3. Now, from each quarter cut V-shaped pieces out in wing or leaf form. Caution: Do not cut too deep!

4. Now fill the cutout apple-blossom petals with chopped pistachio or other nuts. Use whole nuts to represent the stems.

Tip:

With a little imagination, the apple pieces can be used to form other objects. Very simple ones include a butterfly, made by placing two pieces each on the left and right to represent wings and using nuts to form the head, antennae and body. Or for a tulip, put on apple piece on a plate and decorate the stem with pistachio nuts.

Ingredients for one Hedgehog:
1 Pear half from a can
.5 ounces Almond chips
2 Small raisins

Garnishing Tool:
Paring knife

Pears are suitable for decorations whether fresh or cooked. Since fresh pears are not storable for long, it is often simpler to use canned ones. The remaining ones will soon be consumed. Depending on what one wants to decorate, one must remember that, as a rule, fresh, firm pears are slightly sour and cooked pears are very sweet.

Pear Hedgehog

1. Take half a pear out of the can and place it on the work surface with the cut side down.

2. Roast the almond chips in a pan without fat. Be sure to stir the pieces constantly with a wooden spatula. When the pieces show a golden brown color, immediately pour them onto a paper towel, as they will turn black under more heat.

3. Spike the rounded side of the pear half with the roasted almond chips. Carve the narrow end of the pear to form the hedgehog's face.

4. Use the knife to cut two small holes in the face for the eyes.

5. Make two raisins fairly round and push them into the two eyeholes.

Kiwi & Pineapple

Ingredients for 6 Kiwi Crowns:
3 Kiwis
3 Purple grapes
1 Small blue cheese
some parsley
1 Lichee nut

Garnishing Tools:
Zigzag cutter
Paring knife

Kiwis give an exotic touch to decorations. Make sure the fruits to be used have the right degree of ripeness. If they give slightly to finger pressure and the pulp is light green, they are just right. If you use kiwis in combination with dairy products, the foods will taste slightly bitter. Thus scald the kiwis first with hot water, so that the enzyme actinidin loses its effect.

Kiwi Crowns

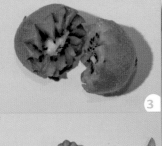

1. Pour hot water over the kiwis and then chill them. Draw a line around the middle of each kiwi with a soft pencil. Do not peel them!

2. Cut along the marked line with the zigzag knife, cutting in to the center.

3. Twist the two halves of the kiwi away from each other and part them.

4. Even the bottoms of the resulting kiwi crowns with the paring knife, so they will stand better.

5. Halve the grapes and remove any seeds.

Cut the cheese into small triangles. Pinch pieces off the parsley. Now garnish the crowns with cheese, grapes, parsley, and the opened lichee nut.

Tip:

If you do not have a zigzag cutter handy, you can also cut the fruit in zigzag form with the paring knife.

Ingredients for 2 Pineapple Halves:
1 Pineapple
2 Kiwis
1 Star fruit
1 Basket of raspberries
1 Banana
A few grapes
1 Orange
1 Apple
A few Peruvian ground cherries
A few lichee nuts
Lemon juice
Sugar
Honey or syrup
Roasted almond chips (optional)

Garnishing Tools:
Chef's knife
Paring knife
Kitchen brush

The queen of tropical fruits cannot bear coldness. Store the fruit at about 18 degrees C. Cut-up fruits belong in the refrigerator. When preparing milk dishes or sweets with pineapple and gelatin, you should always turn to canned fruit, since the gelatin will not become firm otherwise and the dairy foods will taste bitter. In cooking, the pineapple enzyme mixture, bromelaine, will be destroyed.

Fruit Salad in Pineapple Bed

1. Cut the pineapple in half lengthwise with the chef's knife, along with the stalk.

2. With the paring knife, carefully cut the pulp out of the halves about .4 inches from the rind, so that the bowl remains smooth.

3. Cut the removed pulp of the pineapple and the other fruits for the salad into pieces as equally large as possible. Separate the orange segments, halve the grapes and remove the seeds. Prepare a fruit salad with all the fruit chunks, lemon juice, and sugar.

4. Brush the hollowed-out pineapple halves with syrup or honey and fill them with the fruit salad.

Tip:

The pineapple should no longer be green, but still nicely firm, and have a fresh green stalk.
Exotic fruits such as star fruit, lichee nuts, and Peruvian ground cherries are an added treat for special occasions. If you wish, add roasted almond chips.

Lemons & Oranges

Lemons cannot be dispensed within garnishing and decorating. If you use the rind, use only untreated lemons, since many lemons are coated with a wax-like protective and conserving layer before being sold.

Lemon Wheels

1. Clean the untreated lemons thoroughly with a clean cloth.

2. Cut narrow strips of the lemon rind away from top to bottom with the channeling knife.

3. Now cut the channeled lemon into thin slices with the paring knife, so that the slices make a good appearance.

4. Remove any seeds and cut into some of the slices from the rind to the middle. Now bend the ends outward and set up/lay out the lemon slices. Garnish them with parsley.

Tip:

Whoever does not have or want a channeling knife should note that many peelers are equipped with a channeling knife on
the side.

Ingredients for 1 Flower:
1 Untreated orange
A few leaves of lemon mint
for garnishing

Garnishing Tools:
Paring knife

Lovely color accents can be created with oranges or mandarins. The rinds are particularly suitable for decorations as they look nice and give off a splendid aroma. These two types of fruit—like all citrus fruits—are also coated with a layer of wax before being sold. Thus you should use only untreated fruits. Oranges with a thin rind are especially well suited for decorations. By slight pressure on the outside, you can find those with a thin rind.

Orange Blossoms

1. First, clean off the untreated orange with a clean cloth. Cut flowerlike strips into the fruit from top to bottom.

2. Now loosen the resulting strips from the fruit and peel them away from the top down, forming a flower.

3. Carefully remove the fruit.

4. Remove any strings and the white skin of the fruit carefully.

5. Cut the orange into slices, turn over the rind and place an orange slice in the middle. Garnish with the lemon mint leaves.

Tip:

Note the thickness of the rind when buying the oranges—those with too-thick a rind are less suitable for this decoration. If no really nice oranges should be available, mandarins are just as useful.

21

Melons

Melons exist in the most varied types and colors. Watermelons have a glistening dark green rind, red pulp, and many seeds which must be removed with a fork from the pulp before using it as garnishing. The pulp of their smaller relative, the honeydew, has seeds only in the center of the fruit and thus is easier to use. The color of the pulp varies in all types of melons, being light green in the honeydew and orange in the cantaloupe.

Filled Melon

1. Mark the center of the honeydew with a soft pencil, best of all with two parallel lines, so that the zigzags are regular.

2. Now place the zigzag cutter at one point on the marked line and stick it into the center of the melon, making the first cut. Continue all around.

3. Twist the two halves slightly against each other and thus loosen them. Flatten the bottom of the melon half to be filled, using a kitchen knife, so it will not tip over, and remove the pulp with a spoon.

4. Halve the watermelon with the chef's knife and carefully remove the seeds from one half. Put the second half aside. Now use the ball scoop, turning it to bring out small balls. Do the same with the top half of the honeydew. Now fill the prepared half of the honeydew with alternating red and yellow balls.

Tip:

You can wrap the other halves of the melons with foil and keep them in the refrigerator one or two days for later use.

Ingredients for 1 Melon Half:
1 Watermelon
26.4 ounces of fresh
Gouda cheese

Garnishing Tools/Materials:
Chef's knife
Ball scoop
Toothpicks
Wood or Shashlik skewer for
making holes

Cheese-Melon Skewers

1. Halve the melon with the chef's knife and remove the seeds carefully from one half. Now use the ball scoop to remove balls from the half without seeds.

2. It is best to have the cheese cut into slices .8 inches thick at the cheese counter of the supermarket. Then you only need to remove the rind at home and cut the cheese into square cubes (.8 x .8 inches).

3. Stick the cheese cubes and the melon balls alternately onto the toothpicks.

4. Now find an orientation point on the other half of the melon and, beginning from there, stick the cheese-melon skewers evenly onto the melon.

Tip:

Since the melon rind is very hard, the cheese-melon skewers can be stuck in more easily if the holes are made in advance with a wood or Shashlik skewer.

Cucumbers

Whether with or without rind, whole or cut, stuffed, grated or sliced, there is scarcely a type of vegetable that has more uses than the cucumber. Since it consists of 97% water, it always tastes fresh and brightens up every plate with its strong green color.

Stuffed Cucumber Towers

1. Cut the cucumber with the paring knife into slices as equally long as possible, with a length of circa 1.1 inches.

2. Cut stripes into the rind of the cucumber pieces with a channeling knife.

3. Now hollow out the cucumber pieces with the smaller end of the ball scoop. Salt and pepper the inside of the cucumber and roll the cutout balls in ground pepper. Put the balls aside.

4. Fill the hollowed cucumber pieces well with meat salad, using a small spoon.

5. Then garnish with dill and place one cucumber ball on top of each one.

Tip:

Curds, soft cheese or a tasty poultry salad are also suitable for stuffing.

Ingredients for 4—6 Rosettes:
1 Cucumber
1 Tomato
1 Twig of dill for garnishing

Garnishing Tools:
Paring knife

Cucumber Rosette

1. Halve a piece of cucumber about 2.4 inches long lengthwise.

2. Cut into the cucumber piece with very fine, somewhat diagonal cuts like a comb.

3. Now bend every other of the resulting strips toward the inside.

4. Cube the tomato finely and stuff the tomato pieces into the bent strips. Garnish with dill.

Tip:

Cucumber and Tomato—the professionals of the garnishing art! The red-green combination inspires the appetite and pleases the eye.

Tomatoes

There are many different types of tomatoes, from the small cherry tomato through the best-known types, such as the plum, to the beefsteak tomato. Make sure that the tomatoes for garnishing are kept cool but not in the refrigerator. In the refrigerator the tomato takes on a glassy look and loses its flavor.

Tomato Rose

1. For one tomato rose you need a very firm tomato, otherwise the skin will tear. Remove the tomato stem.

2. Beginning with the skin at the bottom of the tomato, peel in a single piece in spiral form.

3. First roll the peel spirals tightly together, only a little looser toward the end, forming a nice rose. Then garnish with parsley or a nice lettuce leaf.

Tip:

Keep the peeled tomato for tomato sauce or quarter it, remove the seeds, cut the pulp into small cubes and add to a salad. Well wrapped in foil, it will keep one or two days in the refrigerator.

Ingredients for 7 Fly Mushrooms:

7 Tomatoes
Salt, pepper
2 Balls of mozzarella
Black and green olives
About 30 basil leaves
Balsamic vinegar
Olive oil
Curds or soft cheese for spotting

Garnishing Tools:
Paring knife
Piping cone

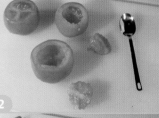

Tomato-Fly Mushrooms

1. Put the tomatoes, as nearly the same size as possible, on the work surface and cut off the upper third of each with the paring knife, as lids. Put the lids aside.

2. Remove the seeds with a ball scoop or teaspoon. Add salt and pepper.

3. Cut the mozzarella into cubes and halve the olives. Mix the mozzarella cubes and olive halves, along with the basil leaves, balsamic vinegar, olive oil, salt and pepper, into a salad in a bowl. Then stuff the salad into the tomato halves.

4. Put the curd or soft cheese into the piping cone and make small dots on the tomato lids.

Tip:

The tomato lids must be completely dry, so the dots do not slide off.

Ingredients for 6—8 Boats:
3 Colorful peppers
1 Small bowl of rice salad (4.4 ounces rice)
1 Spring onion, if you want
A few sprigs of chives for garnishing

Garnishing Tools/Material:
Paring knife
Toothpicks

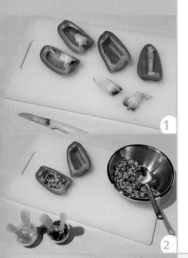

Peppers, with their glowing colors, invite colorful combinations. Whether boats or barrels— they are especially suited for stuffing because of their meager pulp and their firmness.

Pepper Boats

1. Quarter the peppers and remove the cores and white skin. You may want to even up the underside with the paring knife so they stand more securely.

2. Salt and pepper the resulting boats and fill them with rice salad.

3. From the upper part of a spring onion or the unused pieces of pepper, cut out small sails and put them on toothpicks.

4. Now stick the colorful sails onto the stuffed peppers and garnish with chives. Full speed ahead! All seamen, large or small, will be happy to partake of them.

Tip:

If pieces of pepper are left over, simply cube them small and mix them into the rice salad.

The black radish—with its firmness, it is especially suitable for garnishing with nice long spirals. When you shop, make sure that the radish is neither woody nor too soft. It should also have grown very straight. If it has a noticeable green edge when you cut the end off, then peel it until the green is gone. The spiral cutter can otherwise get stuck and cause breakage. Pros work with metal spiral cutters.

Radish Spirals

1. Peel the radish with the peeler and trim off both ends with the paring knife, so that any strings or small woody spots can be removed.

2. Now insert the spike of the spiral cutter into the middle of one end.

3. Twist the cutter evenly into the radish and thus cut it into a spiral.

4. Put the spiral briefly into cold water, so it opens nicely. Take it out and let it dry well, then salt it.

Red Radishes

Ingredients:
1 Bunch of red radishes

Garnishing Tools:
Paring knife

With their fresh consistency, radishes can be worked very well and will stay fresh on a buffet for some time. Make sure that they have a strong red color and are not woody.

Radish Marguerites and Tulips

1. Detach the washed radishes from their leaves. Remove the stems and roots.

2. Then cut into the radishes all around from the top to shortly before the stem attachment (some 10 to 12 times) and peel the red skin away from the white pulp until shortly before the stem attachment.

3. Immediately put the resulting marguerites into cold water to preserve their appearance.

4. To make radish tulips, the radishes are alternately grooved and the pieces are removed.

Ingredients:
1 Bunch of red radishes

Garnishing Tools:
Paring knife

Radish Mice

1. Remove the greens from the radishes. Leave the roots as noses and the stems as tails.

2. Now flatten the radishes slightly on one side, so they stand up properly.

3. Make small ears from the removed pieces and cut holes at the places where the ears should be.

4. Set the ears into the holes and two small cloves into holes as eyes.

Tip:

The radishes should be of varying sizes, to make large and small mice. Choose radishes with long roots, so your mice will have nice long tails.

Carrots

Good-quality carrots have a core that has the same color as the pulp. They do not bend, but must break. Carrots almost always fit into the picture. Whether as bows, bundles or hearts, they form an effective garnish everywhere that will amaze your guests. Carrots are easier to work when they have been blanched first.

Ingredients for some 20 Bows:
1 Carrot
A few chives for garnishing

Garnishing Tools:
Peeler
Paring knife

Carrot Bows

1. Peel the carrots with the peeler and trim off the ends with the paring knife.

2. Now halve the carrot and peel fine strips off lengthwise with the peeler.

3. Cut a small slit, about .4 inches from the edge, on the somewhat wider side of the carrot strips with the paring knife.

4. Now twist the thinner end somewhat and stick it through the slit. This forms a nice bow that you can garnish with the chives.

Tip:

It is best to use just-washed carrots; thus the bows will look best.

Carrot Bundles & Hearts

1. Peel the carrots, and trim off the ends with the paring knife.

2. Now blanch the peeled carrots for five minutes in salted water.

3. Take them out and cut them into equally large pieces about 2.4 inches long. Cut these into fine strips.

4. Pile up some of the strips and cut them into rods. Lay each of the resulting bundles on a chive stalk and carefully tie them together into a bundle.

5. To make small hearts, for example, a soup additive, cut a whole blanched carrot into thin discs and cut the heart shape out of the slice with a cutter. Naturally, you can also use other small cutter shapes.

Tip:

The negative of the heart cutter also makes a nice decoration!

Zucchini

Zucchini has a firmer constituency than, for example, cucumbers. Since they also have fewer seeds and are not so juicy, they are often better suited for garnishing.

Zucchini Bouquets

Ingredients for About 10 Bouquets:
1 Firm, slim Zucchini

Garnishing Tools/Material:
Paring knife
Vegetable slicer
Toothpicks

1. Cut the stem and blossom attachment from the zucchini with a paring knife. Halve the zucchini lengthwise and cut thin slices with the slicer.

2. Cut into one side of the slices like a comb, not too deeply.

3. Roll up the cut slices tightly.

4. Pin the zucchini rolls together with halves of toothpicks. Carefully bend the individual strips a little bit away from each other.

Ingredients for 5—6 Roses:
1 Firm, slim Zucchini

Garnishing Tools/Material:
Paring knife
Vegetable slicer
Toothpicks

Zucchini Rose

1. Cut through the middle of the zucchini.

2. Cut very thin slices with the slicer.

3. Lay out nine equal slices on the table as shown. Beginning from the left, roll the individual slices together. Roll the first two slices quite tightly; then they can be rolled somewhat more loosely.

4. Pin the rolled zucchini leaves together with a toothpick. If the leaves are larger, one can bend them away from each other on top.

5. Cut the bottoms of the zucchini rolls flat, so they will stand up better. With several roses, they can be cut to different heights and placed side by side to decorate a platter.

Tip:

Too many roses do not look very good as a garnish. So if you have a lot of zucchini left over, you can cut it into slices and then halve them. As a garnish for a plate or platter rim, the zucchini semi-circles look very nice.

Leeks & Potatoes

Even if one does not think of garnishing with leeks, they are very suitable for it. They are easy to work with and look nice on the table with their green and white display of colors.

Leek Palm

1. Trim off the green ends and roots from the leek before you wash it.

2. Cut a piece about 4 inches long out of the middle.

3. Cut fine strips from the green end to near the white area.

4. Lay them in cold water at once, so the leek palm opens nicely.

Tip:

Pineapple and leek go well together in both taste and appearance. If you want, place the palm in a piece of pineapple.

The unused pieces of leek can be used for a vegetable soup, etc.

Ingredients for 1 Spiral, 5—6 Slices and 5—6 Balls:
3 Potato
Salt
Frying fat
A few chive stalks, a piece of spring onion or a lettuce leaf for garnishing

Garnishing Tools:
Peeler
Cutting knife
Ball scoop
Potato spiral

The potato—a fine lump that must not always come to the table as a side dish. In our potato ensemble it shows that it can also do a lot as a decoration. Fast-cooking potatoes are best suited for garnishing.

Potato Ensemble

1. Peel the washed potatoes with the peeler and put them in water.

2. Take them out of the water and cut one potato into slices with the slicer. Make small balls of the second potato with the ball scoop.

3. To make a spiral, screw the potato spiral into the long axis of the third potato until the round cutting knife appears at the other end.

4. Turn the spiral slowly backward and pull it out of the potato with light pressure. Then fry the slices, balls and spiral in the fat, one after the other, and then salt them. Garnish with the chives, onions or lettuce.

Tip:

If you like, shake paprika powder onto the potato slices, balls, and spiral after frying. That looks and tastes nice!

The potato pieces left over from the scooping or spiraling can easily be made into mashed potatoes.

Butter

Ingredients for 15—20 Discs:
2 Rolls of butter (4.4 ounces each)
Walnuts or dill to go on them

Garnishing Tools/Material:
Paring knife
Foil
Cutter form

Butter belongs on just about every buffet. But ... do you simply put it there in a butter dish? That looks sort of simple and not decorative. That does not have to be, for decorative things can be conjured up out of our favorite spread. In terms of taste, too, many types can be found in the dairy section of the supermarket, such as salted, herbal or garlic butter.

Butter Discs

1. Cut the ends off the butter rolls and put them aside.

2. Now cut the rolls into coin-thick slices and immediately put them in ice water.

3. When the butter has become firm, put walnuts or dill on some of the discs.

4. Roll out the cutoff ends of the butter roll with a rolling pin under foil.

5. With the cutter, cut any shape you choose, such as a heart, out of the discs and immediately put them in ice water for firmness. Then put the shapes on the rest of the discs.

Tip:

Butter gets soft very quickly. That does not look good and does not have to be. The containers in which the butter is served should be well cooled. Butter remains cool and firm in, for example, a bowl of ice cubes.

Bright Butter Balls & Bands

1. Take the butter packages out of the refrigerator about an hour before you plan to begin working with them. Dip the ball scoop into hot water and press it into one of the butter pieces. Turn out balls and immediately put them in ice water.

2. Meanwhile put the paprika powder, chive pieces, and pepper in small bowls.

3. Take the butter balls out of the water and roll each in one of the three bowls.

4. Dip the butter cutter in hot water and cut off small strips or bands with the rippled side. Put them in ice water immediately, so they stay firm and keep their shape, and do not stick together. Finally, arrange the balls and bands decoratively on a platter and garnish with parsley.

Tip:

For a buffet, it is not easy to determine reliable portions per person, because each person's hunger and taste are different. The composition of the buffet also plays a role. Despite that, one would naturally like to have a guideline to make planning easier. In deciding on quantities of butter, ask yourself what other spreads are offered, such as meat spreads, soft cheese, or margarine. With some .5 ounces per person, you won't go wrong.

Eggs

Ingredients for 6 Roosters:
6 hard-boiled eggs
1 Carrot
1 Red pepper
1 Yellow pepper
12 Black peppercorns
6 Sprigs of dill

Garnishing Tools:
Paring knife
Woden skewer

One always uses hard-boiled eggs for garnishing. Before cooking, they are pierced by an egg-piercer. So the eggs do not explode, you can also put a few drops of vinegar in the water. Chicken eggs are to be cooked about 10 minutes; then they are hard enough. Next they are immediately dipped in cold water, so they can be shelled more easily. Do not cook them too long, or the edge of the egg-white will turn green.

1. Shell the eggs and cut them off flat on the underside, so they will stand by themselves.

2. Peel the carrot and cut lengthwise into pieces about .1 inches thick. Cut the beak out of one piece.

3. From the red pepper, carve the rooster's comb and tail feathers; from the yellow pepper, carve the wings.

4. Cut into the eggs a little at the right places and insert the beak, wings, comb and tail feathers. Carefully make two eyeholes in the egg with the wooden skewer and insert the peppercorns in them. Stick a sprig of dill into the egg over the tail.

Stuffed Eggs

1. Shell the hard-boiled eggs and halve them lengthwise. Remove the yolk from the white with a teaspoon. Put the egg-white halves aside.

2. Press the egg yolks through a fine sieve and mix with the other ingredients for the stuffings. Season with salt and some pepper for a piquant effect.

3. Lay out ten egg halves; add a basil leaf to each. With the piping bag and star or flat nozzle, add the herb and cheese mixture to these ten halves, then the mustard-mayonnaise mixture to the other ten.

4. Garnish each of the mustard-mayonnaise eggs with a sprig of dill. Cut the olives into fine slices and put one in each of the herb-cheese eggs.

Tip:

Such stuffed eggs are especially good for a cold party buffet. You can, of course, also garnish the stuffing with other ingredients, such as halved cherry tomatoes or small pepper strips. Leftover stuffing also tastes good when spread on a piece of toast or baguette.

Aspic

To prepare aspic dishes, use metal or glass pans with fruits, vegetables, meat, poultry, etc., pouring on still-liquid jelly and cooling until the jelly hardens completely in the refrigerator. Then dip the pans briefly in hot water and tip the aspics onto plates. The secret of stability of the forms is the odorless, tasteless gelatin. This "cement" can be made tasty by adding fruit juice or broth. Gelatin is not suitable for vegetarian dining, as it is derived from animal parts.

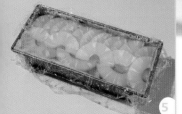

1. Open the pear, peach, and mandarin cans and drain the fruits in a sieve. Drain the fluid of the pineapple and mushrooms separately. Save the fluids. Soften the gelatin in cold water.

2. Dissolve the sugar in warm water in a pot on the stove until no more crystals are visible. Mix the white wine in a bowl with the dissolved sugar, Cointreau, and the opera, peach and mandarin fruit juices.

3. Line the pan smoothly with foil—even the corners should be as crease-free as possible. Cut the peaches into slices and put them in, then the mushrooms and other fruits in layers, contrasting their colors. If necessary, cut the pieces smaller.

4. Take the gelatin out of the water, squeeze briefly and warm briefly on the stove along with a quarter of the fruit-juice mixture until it is completely dissolved. Do not let it get too hot! Take the dissolved gelatin from the stove and carefully stir in the rest of the fruit juice mixture with a brush.

5. Pour the prepared fluid over the fruits in the pan as quickly as you can, and bump the pan on the table several times, so that air caught in the spaces can escape. Chill in the refrigerator for at least four to six hours. Then invert the pan carefully and let the contents come out. Remove the foil. Garnish with colorful fruits such as currants, blackberries, grapes, or ground cherries.

Ingredients for one Bread Pan:
2 Red peppers
1 Zucchini
8 Carrots
8.8 Ounces chicken breast
1 Small package of TK broccoli rosettes
1 Small package of TK cauliflower rosettes
15 Leaves gelatin (.9 ounces in all)
13.5 Ounces chicken broth
1 Small can princess beans, chive rolls and 1 zucchini for garnishing

Garnishing Tools:
Bread pan (ca. 10 x 4 inches)
Foil
Channeling knife

Vegetable and Poultry Tureen

1. Preheat the oven to 250 degrees C. Halve the peppers, clean, remove seeds, and bake the halves about ten minutes. Then lay a damp cloth over them, then peel them. Blanch the zucchini and cleaned carrots in boiling water. Cook the chicken breast in salted water for about 15 minutes. Pour the frozen vegetables into a sieve and let them thaw. Soften the gelatin in cold water.

2. Line the bread pan smoothly with foil—even the corners should be as crease-free as possible. First put the blanched carrots on the bottom, side by side, then cut the cooked chicken breast into strips and place on top the carrots.

3. Halve the blanched zucchini, lay it on the chicken breast, and fill the spaces with the defrosted cauliflower and broccoli rosettes. Finally put the skinned pepper halves on top.

4. Take the gelatin out of the water, squeeze briefly and warm on the stove along with a quarter of the chicken broth until it is completely dissolved. Do not let it get too hot! Take the gelatin from the stove and carefully stir in the rest of the chicken broth with a brush.

5. As quickly as you can, pour the prepared liquid over the vegetables in the pan, and thump it on the table several times, to let remaining air escape from the spaces. Chill in the refrigerator at least four to six hours. Then carefully slide the vegetable-poultry tureen out of the pan and remove the foil.

With a channeling knife, cut even strips from the zucchini rind, then cut off a few slices. Decorate the tureen with the zucchini strips and slices plus the chive rolls. To serve on plates, cut slices about .6 inches thick from the tureen and garnish with zucchini slices, princess beans and chives.

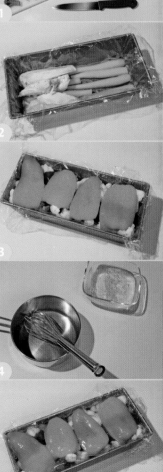

Pastries

It does not always have to be baguettes or bread in its classic form that you serve with foods. Here, too, you can use unusual bread shapes to vary the servings and let your creativity loose with the most unusual types of pastry.

1. Cut strips 4 inches wide from a roll of baking paper and cut them in half diagonally. Wrap a piece around each clay pot.

2. Trim off the projecting paper from the top and bottom rims and put the paper roll in the clay pots.

3. Now put each clay pot on a scrap of baking paper and draw a circle around it with a pencil.

4. Cut the bottoms a little smaller and place them in the pots.

5. Then fill them with the bread dough and sprinkle with the seeds as you wish.

Tip:

It is important that you first dampen the clay pots well in advance. Ideally, pour hot water over them and let them stand in water overnight. Thus they can absorb sufficient moisture, and the bread will be especially juicy. As a tasty alternative, you can also bake sweet buns or cake dough in them.

Puff-Pastry Twists

1. Roll out the puff-pastry dough and cut into strips about .4 inches wide with the paring knife. Lay two strips beside each other in V formation and press the two upper ends together slightly.

2. Make a queue of the two strips and press firmly together at the ends.

3. Lay two more strips on the table so that they cross in the middle, leaving four ends, 1, 2, 3, and 4.

4. Take end 1 in your left and 2 in your right hand. Put 2 on Place 1 and 1 on Place 2. Then take 3 in your left and 4 in your right hand. Place 4 on place 3 and 3 on Place 4. Repeat until all the strips are completely worked. Press the finished queues firmly together at the ends

5. Preheat the oven to 200 degrees C and place the twists on a cookie sheet lined with baking paper. Coat the queues with some beaten egg and sprinkle with caraway, pizza herbs, coarse salt, or sesame.

   Bake the twists 20 minutes and then allow to cool on a rack.

Canapes

Ingredients:
Cantaloupe
Edam cheese chunk
Cherry tomatoes

Lettuce
Camembert cheese
Blackberries
Round pumpernickel

Toast bread
Green peppers
Carrots
Edam cheese, sliced
Chives
Cress

Mozzarella balls
Basil
Cherry tomatoes
Fresh-ground black pepper

Garnishing tools/Material:
Paring knife
Toothpicks
Cutters

These little bite-size morsels generally consist of bread or crackers with meat, fish, cold cuts, eggs or cheese and topped with spicy additions. Canapes are served as finger food without utensils and thus go best as stand-up food for receptions and cocktail parties. So always be sure that the canapés do not get too big. Toothpicks are useful aids, not only for garnishing but also for eating. For four people you need some five to ten canapés, though this depends on what else you offer your guests.

Canapes with Cheese

1. Cut small cubes of cantaloupe pulp, and cheese cubes of the same size. Skewer a melon cube, then a cheese cube, and last a cherry tomato on a toothpick.

2. Tear several leaves of lettuce into small pieces. Cut the Camembert into slices about .2 inches thick and shape them with a small cutter. Arrange a piece of lettuce, a blackberry and a piece of Camembert on a slice of pumpernickel.

3. Cut the toast into small squares. Quarter the peppers and cut them into strips 1.2 inches long. Blanch the carrots and cut into thin slices. Cut the Edam cheese into strips 1.1 inches wide. On each piece of toast put a strip of pepper, a rolled-up slice of cheese and a carrot slice. Push a chive through each cheese roll and sprinkle some cress on the canapes.

4. Skewer a small mozzarella ball, basil leaf, cherry tomato, another basil leaf and a second mozzarella ball in order on a toothpick. For variety, you can also try the following order: tomato, basil, mozzarella, basil, tomato.

Finally, garnish the canapé platter with chives and sprinkle ground pepper along the edges.

46

Canapes with Fish

1. Skewer a ground cherry with leaves and a shrimp on a banana slice.

2. Cut a flower and a small circle out of a pumpernickel slice. Put the crab-soft cheese crème into the piping bag and, with a hole nozzle, squeeze a dot onto each pumpernickel flower. Quarter the grapes, set them on the cheese creme, squeeze another cheese dot onto it and set it on the pumpernickel circle.

3. Cut small hearts out of the toast. On each heart skewer a rocket lettuce leaf, a cherry tomato and a piece of trout fillet.

4. Cut small hexagons out of the black bread and put a piece of Oakleaf lettuce on each. Put the horseradish soft cheese in the piping bag with star nozzle and squeeze a dot onto the lettuce leaf. Cut the salmon into strips and roll up into rosettes. Place a rosette on each cheese dot.

Tip:

For decoration, you can carve small fish out of cantaloupe and make their eyes of dried pink berries, pleasing the eye as well as the taste.

Ingredients:

Black bread
Honeydew melon
Soft cheese
Parma ham
Basil

Black bread
Grapes
Trout slices
Currants

Toast
Salted butter
Green salad
Salami slices
Corn ear

Black bread
Mushrooms
Carrots
Salt, pepper
Vinegar, oil
Lyon sausage
Parsley

Garnishing tools/Material:

Various cutters
Piping bag with star nozzle
Toothpicks
Paring knife
Channeling knife

Canapes with Sausage

1. Cut small flowers out of the black bread and melon. Put the soft cheese in the piping bag with star nozzle and squeeze onto the black bread. Skewer a lemon seed and a roll of ham on the cheese. Finally stick a basil leaf on each toothpick.

2. Cut small hexagons out of the black bread and skewer a grape, a piece of sliced trout and three red currants on each.

3. Cut small hearts out of the toast and spread them with salted butter. Then lay a small piece of lettuce on each heart. Cut to the middle of the salami slices, roll each into a small cone and put one on each lettuce leaf. Put the tip of a corn ear into each salami cone.

4. Cut small hexagons out of the black bread. Cut the mushrooms into slices. Blanch the carrots, cut even grooves into them with the channeling knife, and cut the carrots into slices. Season the mushroom and carrot slices with salt and pepper and then sprinkle with vinegar and oil. Put one mushroom and two carrot slices on each piece of bread. Cut the Lyon into strips, roll them up and put them on the carrots with some parsley.

Ingredients:
Mini-meatballs from the free-zer
Zucchini
Cherry tomatoes

Turkey cutlets
Salt, pepper
Radishes
Chives

Breaded TK poultry sticks
Pineapple
Grapes
Mandarins
Red currants

Pork loin
Salt, pepper
Salad cucumber
Soft herb cheese
Radishes

Garnishing tools/Material:
Vegetable slicer
Paring knife
Toothpicks
Cutters
Party skewers made of metal
Piping bag with round nozzle

Canapes with Meat

1. Fry the mini-meatballs and the chicken sticks well. Season the pork loin with salt and pepper and fry several minutes on all sides. Fry the thin turkey breast briefly on both sides and then season strongly with salt and pepper.

2. Cut thin lengthwise strips from the zucchini with the vegetable slicer, roll them up and skewer each to a mini-meatball along with a cherry tomato.

3. Cut hearts out of the turkey cutlets, decorate each with a radish slice and some chives.

4. Cut the chicken sticks into pieces about 1.6 inches long. Skewer a piece of pineapple, a grape, a mandarin section and a currant to each, using the metal skewers.

5. Cut the pork loin into slices about .8 inches thick. Halve the slices and set them on the cut surface. Put a cucumber slice on each. Put the soft cheese into a piping bag with round nozzle, make a dot on each cucumber slice, and set a radish slice into the soft cheese.

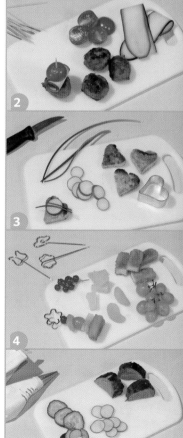

Marzipan

Ingredients for 3 Roses and 3 Leaves:
1.8 ounces marzipan
.9 ounces powdered sugar
Red and green food coloring

Garnishing tools/Material:
Foil
Paring knife

To be able to work the marzipan you get from the supermarket, you must knead it with finely sieved powdered sugar. Always do this with a ration of two parts marzipan to one part powdered sugar. You can color marzipan with food coloring or cocoa powder. Be sure that the colors do not become too strong. You can make figures of marzipan or roll it out and cut it with cutters. Give free rein to your imagination!

Marzipan Rose

1. Knead the marzipan with the finely sieved powdered sugar on a clean work surface.

2. Press half of the marzipan flat and add a little red food coloring. Knead the mass well until it is a soft rose color. Press the remaining marzipan flat, put a little green food coloring on it, and knead well.

3. Roll out the rose marzipan to an even strand about .4 inches thick.

4. Cut pieces about .2 inches long from the strand, and shape them by hand into round balls.

5. For a rose, flatten seven or eight balls on the work surface with a rolling pin.

6. Put the flattened balls on top of each other offset and roll them together into a rose.

7. Press the lower end of the rose together firmly, so it will not fall apart. Make two more roses.

8. Shape one piece of green marzipan into a seamless ball. Make it a little more pointed at one end.

9. Press the ball flat on the work surface with the rolling pin.

10. With a knife, make small indentations in the form of leaf veins on the leaf, and curve the leaf slightly. Make two more leaves. Combine the roses and leaves into a pretty composition.

Tip:

All good things come in threes! Don't just arrange one rose on a cake or tart. It can become inconspicuous. With three you will make a nice impression.

The rest of the marzipan-sugar mixture, which you will want to keep for later, should always be wrapped in foil, so the material will not dry out.

Marzipan and its Relatives

Marzipan

Marzipan is made of sugar and ground almonds. Sometimes rose water or other ingredients are added. Its quality depends above all on the goodness of the prepared almonds and the fineness of the marzipan mass.

Persipan

Since almonds are an expensive raw material, a good substitute for marzipan has been sought. It was found in persipan or parzipan. It is very similar to marzipan, but dies not have its high quality. It also has a somewhat different taste, for it not made of almonds, but of apricot or peach pits.

Turron

Turron contains almonds, sugar, honey, and egg white. Other possible ingredients are chocolate, candied fruits, or peanuts. It has been made in Spain since the sixteenth century, and was brought to Iberia by the Moors from the Arabian area. Turron is a traditional Christmas delicacy in Spain, comparable with out Christmas cookies.

Halva

Sesame seeds are used to make halva. It comes from India and Persia but is also popular in Poland, Greece, and Turkey. In Russia it is usually made of sunflower seeds.

Chocolate

To prepare chocolate as a covering, raised form or squeezed motif, it must be tempered. Do not despair at the first attempts! Tempering the topping requires some practice and experience, but then the results that you get with bought, machine-made products will not be comparable.

Ornaments

1. Pour out the shade morellos. Stir some 1.7 ounces of the poured-out cherry juice along with the cornstarch with a brush until it is free of lumps. Bring the sugar and the rest of the juice to a boil in a pot, stir in the starch mixture with the brush, and let it come to a boil again. Add the morellos. Beat the Mascarpone about 3 to 5 minutes with a hand beater until it is very foamy. Gradually add all the other ingredients for the crème and stir together. Place the crème in the piping bag with the round nozzle and fill it into glasses, alternating with the cherries. Let it chill in the refrigerator for about an hour.

2. Break the chocolate into large pieces, put 2/3 of it in a small dry bowl and place this is a hot water bath. The topping must not be heated over 50 degrees C. As soon as the topping has completely liquefied—meanwhile stir it often—take the bowl out of the water bath and add the remaining, still-solid topping. Dissolve this in the liquid topping while stirring. Then warm the topping carefully in the water bath until it has reached a temperature of ca. 32 degrees C. Take the bowl out of the water bath and add the cherry brandy to the topping. Thus the topping will become harder as it cools.

3. Copy the ornament drawings from the opposite page or download them from the Internet (www.edition-xxl.de/garnieren) and print them out. Lay the printout under a piece of parchment paper. Fasten the parchment paper with a piece of adhesive tape, so it will not slide.

4. Put the chocolate in a prepared piping cone, cut off the point with scissors at the desired width, and follow the ornament pattern with the topping. It is best to start the cone at the lowest point of the ornament, press lightly on the cone and then lift it up. Then lay out the pattern with the resulting lines. Do not hold the point of the cone too close to the parchment paper, otherwise you will not see what you are making. Let the ornaments set about 15 minutes. If the ornaments do not become firm, the topping was used too warm.

5. Carefully loosen the ornaments from the parchment paper with a spatula or paring knife and place them on blobs of cream on the dessert as decorations.

Tip:

You can easily make ornaments a few days in advance. Just be sure to keep them cool.

Chocolate should not be heated over the melting point of 33 degrees C (for milk toppings, 32 degrees C), otherwise it will be discolored, turning grayish. Then the fat rises in the cocoa butter to the surface of the topping and is deposited there. The optimal working temperature is between 30 and 33 degrees C..

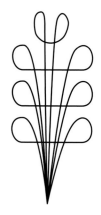

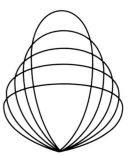

To make a topping with a nice gloss, you must also make sure that the difference between the temperature of the chocolate and the room temperature stays between 10 and 13 degrees C. That means that the ideal room temperature is about 20 degrees C.

If the difference is less than 10 degrees C, the chocolate looks dull—if the difference is more than 13 degrees C, a white-looking coating can form on the surface.

Chocolate Glaze & Powdered Sugar

Ingredients:
7 ounces white chocolate glaze
7 ounces brown chocolate glaze
17.6 ounces strawberries
1 block prepared chocolate mousse, white and brown
chopped pistachio nuts

Garnishing tools:
Paring knife

Chocolate glaze—also called fat glaze—does not need to be tempered, unlike Couverture chocolate, but is tasty and qualitatively not as expensive. Chocolate glaze consists of cacao with the oil removed, plus sugar. Instead of cocoa butter, it contains hardened plant fats. It is not used to make ornaments, but is intended rather for use in simpler desserts.

Chocolate Strawberry Dream

1. Cut the chocolate glaze small with the paring knife and warm it separately in a water bath. Slowly melt it at about 50 degrees C; do not let it get hot.

2. Dip the washed and cleaned strawberries halfway into the liquid chocolate and place them on a piece of baking paper to dry.

3. Put the block chocolate on the table and hold it firmly with one hand. Then cut off chocolate shavings with the paring knife or the back of the knife.

4. Take the mousse from the refrigerator, dip a tablespoon in hot water, and scoop out nice dumplings.

   Place the strawberries around the mousse and sprinkle small bits of pistachio behind them. Finally, carefully sprinkle the chocolate shavings on the mousse.

Tip:

If chocolate-covered strawberries are left over, simply put them on wooden skewers and they will make fruit treats for children, for between meals or for the next day.

Ingredients:
Powdered sugar
Prepared chocolate pudding
3.5 ounces white chocolate glaze
Fruits such as ground cherries or strawberries as garnish (optional)
Garnishing tools:
Thin cardboard
Cutters
Piping cone

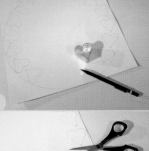

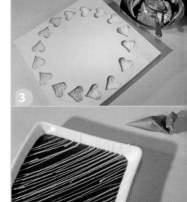

Making a nice plate decoration does not take much. Powdered sugar or cocoa powder is almost always on hand, some thin cardboard, scissors and a pencil or pen. Seek and you will find. Christmas cookies, an ivy leaf or a nice spoon—whatever looks nice and can be used as a pattern will do.

Plate Decorations with Powdered Sugar

1. Make a stencil from the desired shape, that is, place the object on a sufficiently large piece of cardboard (bigger than the plate) and trace it.

2. Cut into the shape carefully and cut it out precisely.

3. Put the stencil on the plate, dust with powdered sugar, and then remove it carefully.

4. Fill the prepared chocolate pudding into the shells and let it cool. Heat the chocolate glaze in a water bath and fill the piping bag with it. Moving from left to right, make a stripe pattern on the pudding.

5. Now put the chocolate pudding on the powdered plate and place a few tasty fruits on it as an ornament.

Tip:

The stencil should always be larger than the object on which it is used, so that it can easily be removed and will not wipe out the plate decorations in the process.

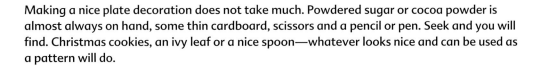

Sugar

Sugar glazes are used on festive cakes and tarts as well as on cookies and muffins. They offer optical variety, and also protect the baked goods from drying out. You can either buy prepared products from the supermarket or very simply make the glaze yourself with some powdered sugar, water, and lemon juice.

Muffins with Glaze

1. Mix the ingredients for the dough, except the cocoa powder, with a hand mixer, and fill six recesses in the muffin sheet 2/3 full. Stir the remaining dough with some cocoa powder and put it in the other recesses on the sheet. Bake 20 minutes at 180 degrees C in a preheated oven. After baking, let cool for about four minutes and take the muffins out of the sheet, letting them cool further on a rack. Meanwhile stir the powdered sugar, lemon juice and two tablespoons of water with a spoon in a small bowl to a smooth glaze.

2. Use a fork to dip two light and two dark muffins upside down in the sugar glaze, or coat them with a kitchen brush.

3. Also put some glaze in a piping bag and make zigzag lines on the other four dark muffins.

4. Add some food coloring, such as red, to the rest of the sugar glaze, stir it well, and coat the last four dark muffins with it.

5. Let the glaze dry slightly and decorate the muffins as you wish, with Smarties, nuts, sugar figures, cherries, or lemon mint.

Ingredients für 4 Panna Cotta:

For the panna cotta sauce:
7 leaves gelatin (.4 ounces)
17 ounces sweet cream
5.3 ounces sugar
.7 ounces cherry brandy

For the orange sauce:
.7 ounces cornstarch
2.3 ounces sugar
8.5 ounces orange juice
A dash of Cointreau

For the sugar grid:
8.8 ounces sugar
Some oil

Garnishing tools/Material:
4 Cups
Paring knife

Panna Cotta with Sugar Grid

1. Soften the gelatin in cold water, heat the cream in a pot and let it reduce somewhat. Add the sugar, squeeze out the softened gelatin and add to the boiling cream. Stir well and take the pot off the stove. When the liquid has cooled, add the cherry brandy, stir well again and pour into the cups. Put the dessert in the refrigerator for at least an hour and a half. Then let some hot water run into the sink and put the cups in individually. After about 30 seconds take the cups out and remove the dessert from the cup. Help it along with the paring knife if necessary. Let the Panna Cotta dry somewhat, put it on a cutting board, and refrigerate again.

2. For the sugar grid, caramelize the sugar in a pot over medium heat, stir constantly with a spoon and let it cool somewhat.

3. Spread a sheet of aluminum foil and brush with oil. Dip a fork into the sugar and move quickly to form lines from left to right and then from bottom to top over the foil. Let it cool.

4. For the orange sauce, pour the cornstarch into a small bowl. Now add the sugar and stir smooth with some 8.5 ounces of orange juice. Boil the rest of the orange juice and stir into the dissolved cornstarch. Let it all boil briefly. Then let it cool thoroughly and add Cointreau to taste. Let the sauce cool.

5. Put each Panna Cotta on a plate and pour the sauce with a spoon over the edge of each Panna Cotta. Break four nice pieces off the sugar grid and garnish the dessert with them.

Tip:

Any leftover sugar mass should not be thrown out! It is removed from the pot most easily if you fill the pot to the brim with water and bring it to a boil.

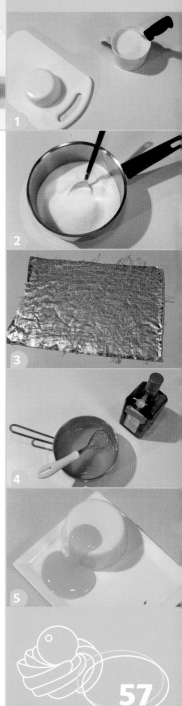

Ingredients:

For the cake:
1 Dark cake bottom

For the filling:
2 Teaspoons cornstarch
1 Jar morello cherries (25.4 ounces, net weight 12.3 ounces)
33.8 Ounces sweet cream
4 Packages cream stiffener
A dash of cherry brandy

For Garnishing:
1 Bar chocolate
16 Shade morello cherries

Garnishing Tools:
Piping bag with star nozzle
Spatula
Cake divider

Always use very fresh cream direct from the refrigerator. Cream stiffener is a small but very fine aid that gives stability to whipped cream for any long cake decoration. But do not put too much of it in the cream; otherwise it will become greasy!

Black Forest Cherry Cake

1. Drain the morello cherries in a sieve and save the juice. Stir the cherry juice with the cornstarch in a pot, add the cherries and bring to a boil until the fruits gel somewhat. Take the pot off the stove and let it cool thoroughly. Take 16 cherries from the pot and put them aside for the decoration. Beat the sauce stiff with cream stiffener and cherry brandy. Put part of it in the piping bag for the garnish. Cut through the biscuit bottom twice. Sprinkle some cherry brandy on the bottom slice, put morello cherries on it and spread some of the cream mixture on it. Put the second slice of cake on this and coat with cream. Put on the third slice and spread the rest of the cream over the whole cake with the spatula. Then gradually ice the sides of the cake.

Let the rim of the cream stand a bit higher than the top of the cake.

2. To finish the top of the cake, smooth the cream from outside to inside.

3. Carefully press the cake divider on the cream.

4. Shave chocolate from the bar over the cake with a knife.

5. With the piping bag and star nozzle, make rosettes on the pieces of cake. Turn the bag in a circle and pull the nozzle away upward under slight pressure. Put one of the 16 cherries on each of the rosettes.

Butter Crème Butterfly

Butter crème is used mainly for coating, filling, and garnishing layer cakes. There are various kinds of butter crème. The French type is easiest to make, thus we have chosen it for this recipe. When making it, you should use only fresh eggs and heat them strongly to rule out the carrying of salmonella.

Ingredients:

For the cake:
13.2 Ounces sweet cream butter
6.7 Ounces sugar
5 Eggs
Ca. 4 cl. Cointreau
1 Round layer cake bottom

For Garnishing:
3.5 Ounces marzipan
1.8 Ounces powdered sugar
Cocoa powder
8 Sugar flowers

Garnishing Tools:
Cookie sheet
Spatula
Kitchen platter (ca. 14 x 14 in)
Garnishing comb
Piping bag with round and star nozzles

1. Beat the soft butter to a foam with the hand mixer for about ten minutes. Stir sugar and eggs in a bowl and heat to about 85 degrees C. in a water bath, stirring constantly with a brush. Caution: Don't let it boil, or the eggs will run! Take the bowl out of the water bath and beat to a foam again with the hand mixer, until no more warmth can be felt. Gradually add the foamy butter material, stirring constantly. Finally add Cointreau drop by drop. Cut the cake bottom twice. Lay the first piece on the cookie sheet and cover thinly with crème, using the spatula. Put the next cake layer on it and sprinkle with somewhat thinned Cointreau. Spread crème on it and put on the last layer. First spread the crème on the top and sides, and then smooth it. Cut the cake in half in the middle and place the halves back to back on the kitchen platter. Run the garnishing comb along the edge.

2. Knead the marzipan with the sieved powdered sugar, press it flat, sieve some cocoa powder over it and knead it well. Make a tail and two antennae. Cut small grooves in the tail with a knife.

3. Put some of the crème in the piping bag with the round nozzle. Garnish the wings with curving bands.

4. With the piping bag and star nozzle, put a rosette at the end of each antenna.

5. Color the rest of the butter crème brown with some sieved cocoa powder. With the piping bag and star nozzle garnish the outer edges of the wings with rows of small dots, the inner, using the round nozzle, with two smaller curved lines. Set the sugar flowers on the wings and antennae.

Sauce Plates

Ingredients:
1 Cup sour cream
A little Milk
1 Small glass currant jelly
Strawberries and mint leaves

Garnishing Tools:
Piping cones
Wooden skewer
Cocoa sprinkler

You can bring any dessert to a high gloss with a sauce mirror. It is best to make it on a big flat one-colored plate, using two different-colored sauces. First set up the sauce mirror and then decorate it. You can arrange fruits, parfaits, poured crèmes, ice cream or even tureens optimally on it.

Sauce Hearts, Magic Flowers & Spirals

1. Thin the sour cream with the milk, so that it has a sauce-like creamy consistency. Note: Do not thin it too much!

2. Strain the currant jelly through a sieve to remove any lumps. Thin it with some water to make it softer.

3. At each corner of a square plate, use a teaspoon to make a round disc of sauce, using the thinned cream. Put the currant jelly in a prepared piping cone and make three dots in a row on the discs.

4. Run the dull side of the wooden skewer from the rim of the plate to the middle through the dots, so that they take on a heart shape. Make curved lines in the empty spaces with the currant jelly. Strew a little cocoa powder from the cocoa sprinkler onto a piece of paper until the cocoa powder comes out smoothly. Then sprinkle it lightly on the corners of the plate.

Quarter a strawberry, but do not cut all the way through it, so that it makes a flower shape. Put a mint leaf in the middle of the strawberry. Quarter a second strawberry completely and place the pieces around the strawberry flower in star form.

5. With the same ingredients you can also make other sauce mirrors, such as the magic flower. Proceed at first as in 1 and 2. Then make a disc of thinned sour cream in the middle of a round plate. Put currant jelly in a piping cone and make a spiral on the disc.

6. Draw the dull side of the skewer from the middle to the edge of the plate at four equal intervals. Do the same four more times at intervals of one-eighth, from the edge to the middle.

Cut about four strawberries into eighths and arrange them in a fan shape around the sauce mirror. Arrange four mint leaves symmetrically around the strawberry fan and use the cocoa sprinkler to create fine color accents on the edge of the plate.

7. Another sauce pattern, the spiral, is made by making one circle each of sour cream stripes with two different piping cones. Here the outer one is made of sour cream and the inner one of currant jelly.

8. Now run the dull side of the skewer through both sauces in circular movements, making a wavy pattern.

Put a strawberry flower in the center of the plate. Quarter two more strawberries and place them alternately on their upper and undersides around the flower. Garnish the plate decoratively with a few mint leaves and the cocoa sprinkler.

Plate Decorations

Ingredients:
Sushi for the desired number of people (ca. 8-10) pieces per person if it is a main course, about half of that as an appetizer), for example, Salmon Nigiri, Giant Shrimp Nigiri, Salmon Maki, Cucumber Maki, California Rolls
1 Carrot
A few chive stalks
Wasabi paste
Inlaid ginger
Soy sauce
Fortune cookies (optional)

Garnishing Tools/Material:
Paring knife
Flower-shape cookie cutter with ejector
Chopsticks for the desired number of people

If you would like to place foods individually at each place setting on the table or in a buffet, you can do this using one or several plates. Always make sure what kinds of food are involved. For example, an appetizer is arranged differently from a warm dish. There are no limits to the variety. The unbeatable advantage of one plate over a platter in a buffet is that it can be exchanged more often, letting the buffet look fresh longer!

Sushi

Preparing sushi requires some practice. But if you want to prepare bought sushi quickly for several guests, make sure that you never let it stand too long uncooked. For example, do not put it on a big platter in a buffet, but always supply small portions over and over.

1. Steam several carrot slices and cut flower designs on them with the filigree cutter with ejector.

2. Simulate small flower stalks with two short chive stalks. Have them start at the edge of the plate. Set a Wasabi dot from the tube over the lower ends of the stalks. Caution: very spicy!

3. Arrange the sushis on the individual plates, always in a line, and put the inlaid ginger on the plate. This will be eaten between the individual sushis to refresh the gums.

4. Pour some soy sauce into a small, shallow dish for each guest. According to taste and desired spiciness, each one can stir some Wasabi paste in the sauce. Also include chopsticks to create the right Japanese ambiance. Arrange the plates symmetrically to each other—simple Asiatic elegance, the character of which can be emphasized with fortune cookies.

Tip:

Green tea in bowls makes an appropriate drink.

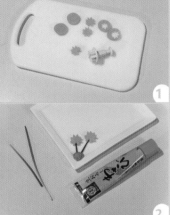

Ingredients for about

4 People:
14.1 Ounces raw ham slices, air-dried
1 Honeydew melon
17.6 Ounces green seedless grapes
8.8 Ounces oval cherry tomatoes
Basil
2 Fresh, firm figs
Butter
1 Small French bread loaf

Garnishing Tools:
Zigzag cutter
Paring knife
Butter knife

Ham Platter

1. Arrange the ham slices loosely on a small plate. Use a ball scoop to make four or five balls of honeydew, and place them in the middle.

2. Remove the grapes from their stems and put them in a small dish. In a dish of the same size put the oval cherry tomatoes and garnish them with basil.

3. Cut a zigzag around the middle of the fig, and separate the two pieces by twisting slightly. With the butter knife, take two rolls of butter and arrange them on the plate along with three slices of the bread and one fig half.

Tip:

The size and shape of the plate depend on the types and quantities of the foods placed on it. The dishes should always have sufficient space for the foods, for an overloaded plate looks overdone and unattractive. But not only the choice of plates is important; so is their arrangement relative to each other. With just a little effort, an imposing appetizer is created.

Ingredients for 6 People:
1 Oakleaf lettuce
1 Orange
5 Slices smoked cheese
6.3 Ounces French soft cheese, rolls 2 inches in diameter
7 Slices butter cheese
10.6 Ounces chunk of Swiss cheese
5.3 Ounces camembert with peppercorns
6 Slices mozzarella
3 Triangles camembert
3.5 Ounces chunk of brie
3 Kiwis
1 Zespri
2 Fresh figs
1 Bunch celery

Garnishing Tools/Material:
Platter (ca. 14 x 20 in)
Paring knife

Before you begin to load a platter, you should first carefully select the shape of the platter and bear in mind the quantity of foods to be placed on it. Place only edible things on platters, no decorations, paper or dummies. Make sure that the foods placed on the platter will stand up to a long period, so the platter will look fresh as long as possible. With a small number of guests—up to about six—there should be something there for everyone.

Cheese Platter

1. Separate the lettuce leaves and make a small pile of them at the upper left corner of the platter. Cut the orange into thin slices and put a few at the opposite corner. Hold three slices back.

2. Lay the smoked cheese slices on the lettuce. Cut the soft cheese roll into pieces and lay them in an arc around the lettuce and smoked cheese. Roll up the butter cheese slices and arrange them so they end at the lower right edge of the platter. Cut the Swiss cheese into pieces and put them between the orange slices and the upper edge of the platter.

3. Cut the camembert with peppercorns into eight equal pieces and place them in star shape in the middle of the platter.

4. In the last empty corner of the platter place the mozzarella slices and camembert pieces. Cut the brie into equal pieces and arrange them on the orange slices. Cut zigzags into the kiwis and figs and pull the halves apart by twisting them slightly. Arrange the kiwi and fig halves decoratively on the platter. Halve the last three orange slices and put them between the butter cheese rolls. Fill small holes with parsley.

Ingredients for 8 People:

For the fish:
1 Lemon
5.3 Ounces mackerel fillet, smo-ked, and with colored pepper
7 Ounces shrimp, cooked and shelled
9.7 Ounces salmon, smoked and with colored pepper
1 Lime
8.8 Ounces trout fillet
3.5 Ounces butter mackerel, smoked
14.1 Ounces salmon in slices
1 Bunch dill

For the stuffed eggs:
5 Hard-boiled eggs
2 Tablespoons of soft cheese
1 Very ripe avocado
1 Teaspoon lemon juice
1 Tablespoon milk

Salt, pepper
Cress

Garnishing Tools/Material:
Round platter ca. 18 in diameter
Channeling knife
Paring knife
Piping bag with star nozzle

Fish Platter

1. Remove strips of the lemon rind lengthwise with the channeling knife. Cut the fruit into very thin slices and put them along the left edge of the platter.

2. Carefully remove the skin from the mak-kerel fillet and cut the fillet into equal pieces. Put the mackerel skin beside the lemon slices and put the mackerel pieces right on top of it. Fill in the lower part of the plate with shrimp.

3. Halve the five hard-boiled eggs and carefully remove the yolks. Push the yolks through a fine sieve, then add the soft cheese, the squeezed fruit pulp of the avocado, lemon juice and milk, and stir it all to a smooth crème with the brush. Flavor to taste with salt and pepper. Put the crème in the piping bag with star nozzle, and fill the egg halves with it. Hold back two halves, so you can put them at the edges the platter with their cut sides down for a better hold. Lay out the stuffed eggs alongside the mackerel fillets. Put a shrimp on every

other egg and scatter cress on all of them. Carefully remove the skin from the smoked salmon, cut the salmon into equal pieces, put it back on the skin and arrange it on the right side of the platter.

4. Cut the lime into thin slices and place them above the salmon.

5. Cut the trout fillet into small pieces and arrange them along the curve of the stuffed eggs. Cut the butter mackerel in pieces and put them in a fan shape bet-ween the trout fillet and the salmon. Fill the two still-empty parts of the platter with slices of smoked salmon. Garnish the lemon and salmon slices with the dill.

Tip:

A good, original alternative to a platter is the back of a serving tray.

Equal and very thin lemon slices can be made with a bread slicing machine.

Drinks

Ingredients for 4 Glasses:
23.7 Ounces milk
8.5 Ounces orange juice
7 Ounces sugar
A Dash of orange syrup

For Garnishing:
Paring knife
Channeling knife
8 Straws
1 Orange

1. Fruity Orange Shake

Blend the ingredients in a blender and carefully fill the glasses about 4/5 full of the finished shake. To decorate a glass, quarter an orange slice and cut halfway into two quarters. Put them on opposite sides of the glass. Cut off the orange peel in spiral form with the channeling knife. Hang the spiral over the edge of the glass and lay two straws atop the glass.

Ingredients for 1 Glass:
1.3 Ounces Campari
Ice cubes

For Garnishing:
Paring knife
1 Orange slice
1 Cocktail umbrella

2. Campari on the Rocks

Cut into the orange slice at one place and stick in a cocktail umbrella. Fill a tall glass with ice cubes and pour the Campari over them. Stick the orange slice on the rim of the glass. Serve at once.

Ingredients for 1 Glass:
1.7 Ounces white rum
1.3 Ounces coconut crème
2.7 Ounces pineapple juice

For Garnishing:
Paring knife
1 Mini-pineapple
1 Cocktail palm
3 Banana slices
2 Cherries

3. Piña Colada

Mix the ingredients for the cocktail thoroughly. Remove two leaves of the mini-pineapple, cut into their lower ends, and stick them on the rim of the glass. Skewer a banana slice, a piece of pineapple, and a cherry on a cocktail palm. Repeat the order until the skewer is full. Carefully pour the cocktail into the glass, to about 4/5 full. Lay the skewer decoratively across the glass.

4. Latte Macchiato

Stir the milk in a small pot on the stove with a milk beater. Pour into a tall glass, make an espresso and slowly, carefully pour it over the milk. Lay the stencil on the glass and dust the surface with some cocoa powder.

Ingredients for 1 Glass:
10.1 Ounces milk (1.5%)
1 Espresso

For Garnishing:
Stencil of your choice
Cocoa powder

5. Sparkling Wine

Cut slightly into two opposite sides of a kumquat and fold the flaps forward as fins. Halve the second kumquat and cut the tailfin out of the skin. Slit the back of the fish slightly and stick the tailfin into the slit. Also cut the dorsal fin out of the second kumquat and attach it to the fish's back. Cut the eyeholes with the paring knife, and stick small pieces of pistachio in. Cut into the fish's belly and stick it on the glass. Fill the glass with sparkling wine.

Ingredients for 1 Glass:
Sparkling wine

For Garnishing:
Paring knife
2 Kumquats
1 Finely chopped pistachio nut

6. Cherry Banana Juice

Spread the sugar on a flat plate. Moisten the rim of the glass and press it upside down on the sugar. Let the sugar on the rim dry somewhat. Stick the banana slices and finally the ground cherry on the wooden skewer. Now pour the banana juice into the glass, and then slowly pour in the cherry juice. Now stick the skewer into the glass and serve the drink.

Ingredients for 1 Glass:
4.2 Ounces banana juice
4.2 Ounces cherry juice

For Garnishing:
1.8 Ounces sugar
2 Banana slices
1 Ground cherry
1 Wooden skewer

Ingredients for 2 Sand Cakes:

For the cakes:
17.6 ounces butter
17.6 ounces cornstarch
2 pinches of salt
10 eggs
17.6 ounces sugar
.4 ounces baking powder

For the garnish:
15.9 ounces brown chocolate glaze
5.3 ounces powdered sugar
7 ounces marzipan
1 package large Smarties
1 package small Smarties
A few carrot tops (not the greens, but the top 2 inches or so of carrots)
A few mini-carrot tops (the top 1.1 inch of smaller carrots)
Cotton wool
3.5 ounces white chocolate glaze

Garnishing tools:
2 loaf pans, 10 x 3.5 inches
Bread knife
Kitchen brush
Paring knife
One large, one small circle cutter
2 piping bags

A tasty cake is part of every child's birthday. If it not only tastes good, but also is garnished right for children, the birthday party is guaranteed to be a big success. For even the smallest children eat with their eyes too!

Tasty Steam Locomotive

1. Mix the ingredients for the cake with a hand mixer and put the dough in the greased loaf pans. Bake 70 minutes at 175 degrees C in a preheated oven. Then put the two cooled cakes on baking paper and cut the ends off evenly with the bread knife. Lay out one of the loaves completely flat. Shorten the other about 1/3 and stand it upright behind the first.

2. Liquefy the brown chocolate glaze in a water bath and apply lavishly with a brush to both cakes. Apply the first layer thin and carefully, and let it dry somewhat. Then put on the second coat as smoothly as you can. Leave some chocolate glaze for the garnishing. Trim the still-soft chocolate along the edges of the cake with a paring knife.

3. Sieve the powdered sugar and knead it with the mass of marzipan. Then roll the mass out .2 inches thick. Use the cutters to make four large and four small circles. Glaze all the carrot tops as well.

4. Use the paring knife to cut two windows, each 1.8 x 2.4 inches out of the marzipan. Make a marzipan strip about .4 inches in diameter. From the strip, make four pieces with a length of ca. .8 inches

each, and make the locomotive's buffers of them. Cut out a strip with a width of about .4 inches.

5. Fill a piping cone with chocolate glaze and decorate the marzipan pieces with dots and lines.

6. Stick the marzipan pieces on with some chocolate glaze, apply Smarties to the locomotive, and attach one large and one small carrot top as smokestacks. Stick the cotton wool to the top of the larger smokestack with chocolate glaze.

7. Liquefy the white chocolate glaze in a water bath and put it in the second piping cone. Lay a few large carrot tops on their sides and make little faces on them with the glaze. Stick a Smartie on each one as the nose. Let them dry sufficiently before setting them up!

8. Put the mini-carrot tops in a clean egg box and make little faces on them as well.

Tip:

You can also make the wheel circles in Step 3 with a large and a small glass.

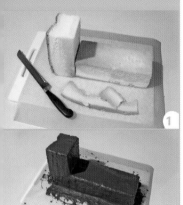

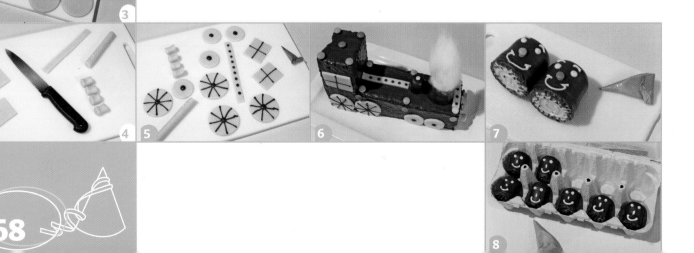

Ingredients for 8—10 People:
1 lemon
1 tomato
1 bunch dill
17.6 ounces fish rolls (10 or 11 pieces)
17.6 ounces Bismarck herring
2 hard-boiled eggs
1 onion
10-11 sour pickles
1 blanched carrot

Garnishing tools/Material:
Channeling knife
Paring knife
Platter (ca. 14 x 20 inches)
Egg slicer
Cutters

The traditional hangover breakfast after a Mardi Gras party! To be sure, it will not substantially ameliorate the aftereffects of excessive alcohol consumption the previous evening, but nothing is better than a sour herring!

German Sushi

1. Cut lengthwise strips of lemon rind with the channeling knife. Cut the fruit into very thin slices with the paring knife and place them to the left and right on the platter. Carve a rose of the tomato and, along with the dill, set it on the upper left edge of the platter.

2. Place the fish rolls in a gentle curve on the platter near the dill.

3. Halve six Bismarck herrings lengthwise, and fan out six halves in the lower right corner of the platter. Make the other six into small rolls and set them on six lemon slices. Put the other six on the lemon slices at the lower left.

4. Slice the eggs into even slices with the slicer and place them to the left and right on the platter.

5. Peel the onion and cut it into fine rings. Put the rest of the dill on the platter between the hard-boiled eggs and the Bismarck herrings, and scatter the onion rings over it.

6. Halve the sour pickles, cut into them lengthwise and make them into fans. Put one fan between each pair of the Bismarck herrings. Fill the space at the right near the fish rolls with the rest of the fans.

7. Cut the blanched carrot into slices and cut flowers out of them with the cutter. Garnish the platter with the carrot flowers.

Tip:

This is best served with French bread and peeled potatoes.

Let the fish dry well in advance, so the juice will not run from the platter. A platter with a juice groove is optimal here.

Ingredients for 1 Bear:

For the bear:
3.5 ounces marzipan
1.8 ounces powdered sugar
1.8 ounces sugar
½ teaspoon cocoa powder
Red food coloring
1.2 teaspoon egg-white
Some chocolate glaze

For garnishing:
21.1 ounces chocolate glaze
1.8 ounces white topping
1 package of white chocolate hearts

Garnishing tools:
Wooden skewer
2 Piping cones
Spatula

February 14 is the lovers' day. Many cards and gifts are exchanged on that day. This cake is a very loving gift: individual, unbelievable, and chocolaty delicious.

Bears with Heart

1. Knead the mass of marzipan with the finely sieved powdered sugar on a clean work surface.

2. Dissolve the sugar in .7 ounces of water under low heat.

3. Make a seamless ball of 1.8 ounces of the marzipan-sugar mixture. Roll the ball into a tapered form that stands straight on its bottom and tilts slightly at the top. Work out the bear's shoulders a little.

4. Press 1.2 ounces of the marzipan flat with your hand and sieve the cocoa powder over it. Knead the whole thing well until it has an even brown color. Press .1 ounce of the marzipan flat and put a little red food coloring on it. Knead this well too, until a soft rose color results.

5. Weigh 1.2 ounces of the brown marzipan and make two seamless balls of .2 ounces each and two more of .4 ounces each out of it. Roll the balls into tapering forms and make the ends stumpy.

6. From the shorter of these pieces, make the arms; from the longer, the legs. Attach them to the bear's body by hand, using sugar water.

7. Make a seamless ball of .5 ounces of the light marzipan. Make the bear's pointed nose on one end and press it in lightly.

8. Make two seamless balls, each of .1 ounces of the dark marzipan, flatten them lightly and make indentations for the ears with the wooden skewer. Attach the ears to the back of the bear's head with sugar water. Make one small ball of the dark marzipan and attach it to the bear's snout. Make holes for the bear's eyes with the skewer.

9. Make a seamless ball of the rose marzipan, Fold it together and make a heart of it.

10. Squeeze egg-white glaze into the bear's eyeholes. For the glaze, mix the egg-white with three tablespoons of powdered sugar until a firm mass results. Make the bear's pupils, finger- and toe-nails of chocolate glaze from the other piping cone.

11. Put the prepared, cooled cake on a cooling rack and slide a piece of baking paper under it. Pour the chocolate glaze steadily over the cake, so that it covers the edge well. Now smooth the surface with a spatula.

Heat the topping in a water bath, put it in a piping cone, and squeeze a flower design only the cake. Place the chocolate hearts on the cake.

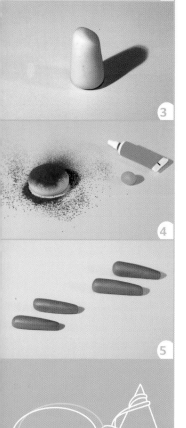

Easter

Combine all the symbols of Easter on one holiday platter: Easter bunny and Easter eggs hidden in a spring meadow. A festive feast that not only tastes good but also pleases—especially children.

Easter Feast

1. Soften the rolls in water. Peel the onions and cut into small cubes. Mix both with the ground meat and season with salt, pepper, and paprika. Grease a baking pan with oil and make a rabbit's head of the ground meat.

2. Preheat the oven and bake the meat ca. 45 minutes at about 200 degrees C, with heat above and below. Take the rabbit head out of the oven and let it cool for a time. Then carefully put it on the plate.

3. Slice the zucchini into long thin slices with the vegetable slicer, and arrange the slices on the platter to the height of the rabbit's ears.

4. Cut one of the blanched carrots into slices and make flowers of them with the cutter. Place the flowers on the zucchini slices. Cut the second carrot lengthwise into thin slices with the vegetable slicer and roll them up into rosettes. Also place these on the zucchini slices. Use the cheese slices to make a bow tie for the rabbit and place it right under his head. Cut all except one-half of the hard-boiled eggs into slices. Use one end piece to decorate the bow tie and put two more aside for the rabbit's eyes. Cut flowers out of the rest of the egg slices. Place a few mint leaves near the carrot roses.

5. Cut two eyes out of the two remaining egg ends and put a pistachio nut in each one as a pupil. For the nose, make a half-moon shape of the remaining cheese and represent his whiskers with a few chives. Put the parsley and the remaining egg half above the rabbit's head.

Ingredients for 6 to 8 people:

For the soup:
2 butternut squash
2 onions
4 garlic cloves
3.5 ounces clarified butter
1 liter meat broth
Salt
Pepper
Nutmeg
3-4 slices toast
1.8 ounces butter
1.8 ounces squash seeds

For the gelatin dessert:
10 leaves gelatin (.6 ounces)
7 ounces sugar
1.7 ounces raspberry spirit
Green food coloring

Garnishing tools:
Small cake pans or plates
Paring knife
Butter shaper

Every year in the night of October 31 to November 1, the haunting begins: Devils, ghosts, vampires and witches with pointed hats and black cats on their shoulder go from house to house. Bewitch your guests with an appropriate meal, watched over by a grisly Jack O' Lantern.

Grisly Meal

1. Soften the gelatin for the pudding in cold water. Boil 17 ounces water and the sugar together. Take from the stove and stir in the dissolved gelatin with a brush. Let it cool somewhat and add the raspberry spirit, stirring. (Caution: Not suitable for children!) Color the mixture with green food coloring. Pour it into small cake forms or cups and let it set in the refrigerator overnight.

2. Pour the gelatin out of the forms. You may help it with a paring knife.

3. Cut a lid from each butternut squash. The rim will be even if you draw a line first with a felt-tip marker.

4. Remove the firm pulp from both squashes. That can be done very well with a butter shaper. Throw away the fibrous and furry pulp; the seeds can be used in other ways.

5. The soup recipe includes about 12.2 pounds of squash pulp. Peel the onions and cut them into fine cubes; peel the garlic cloves. Heat clarified butter in a large pot and steam the onions in it. Squeeze the garlic into the onions with a garlic press and stir constantly. The squash pulp can be cut small and added to the onions in the pot. Stirring constantly, steam it a few minutes. Add

the meat broth and cook the mixture 15 to 20 minutes, until finished. Puree the squash pulp with a magic wand and flavor with salt, pepper and nutmeg. Put the finished soup in the two cleaned-out squashes.

6. Cut the toast into small cubes and brown it with the butter in a pan. Scatter the toast cubes and the squash seeds on the soup.

7. With the lids on, the soup in the squashes will stay hot longer and awakens curiosity among the diners.

Tip:

If you would like to serve the soup to all your six to eight guests, it is best to cook all the pulp of six to eight squash into soup and freeze the leftovers. Another possibility is to serve the soup in nice soup bowls from the start.

A grisly carved Jack O' Lantern pumpkin makes a haunting face at any Halloween buffet. Cut the lid off a pumpkin, draw a face on it, hollow out the pumpkin and cut out the face with a sharp knife. It's frightful!

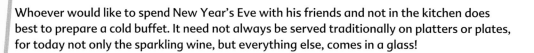

Ingredients for 6 glasses:

Ca. 21.1 Ounces salt
Ca. 10.6 Ounces sugar
4 Slices of cooked ham
4 Grissini
5 Very thin slices of salami
3 Slices of turkey breast
2 Slices of semi-hard cheese
(Tilsit, Gouda, Edam)
1 Blanched carrot
1 Blanched zucchini
4 Long salt rods
6 Mini-Wieners
3.5 Ounces butter cheese
Ca. 20 Grapes
4 Cocktail cherries
5.3 Ounces camembert
1 Honeydew

Garnishing Tools/Materials:

6 Glasses
Paring knife
Wooden skewers
Vegetable slicer
Circular cutter
Straws

Whoever would like to spend New Year's Eve with his friends and not in the kitchen does best to prepare a cold buffet. It need not always be served traditionally on platters or plates, for today not only the sparkling wine, but everything else, comes in a glass!

Party for "Swizzlers"

1. Use just one type of glass if possible, or at least those that harmonize well with each other. Fill the glasses for the zingy skewers about 1/3 full of salt. You can use either fine- or coarse-grained salt. The latter can be had in various forms and gives the skewers in the glasses a very steady hold.

2. For the sweet skewers, one can fill the glasses 1/3 full of sugar. The classic white or brown sugar can be used. Whoever wants more color can used colored sugar, as it is available in several colors, such as blue, yellow, or orange.

3. Fold the ham slices together in the middle lengthwise. Make several cuts into the middle about 1.2 inches apart and skewer them on the breadsticks. Put the finished breadstick skewers right into the glasses.

4. Fold the salami slices together in the middle and make several cuts at .8-inch intervals. Skewer the slices on the wooden skewers and put them right in the glasses.

5. Likewise cut slits in the turkey breast and semi-hard cheese with the knife and put them on wooden skewers. If the slices do not make any nice waves, simply double them.

6. Slice the blanched carrot and zucchini lengthwise with the vegetable slicer, make slits in them, and put them on long salt rods. First dry the slices well with paper towels, so the salt rods do not soften. Put the salt-rod skewers in the glasses.

7. Mixed variations of mini-Wieners, butter-cheese cubes, grapes, cherries, and camembert can also be made up and placed in the glasses.

8. Scoop small balls out of the melon and alternate them with grapes on the straws. The melon balls should not be too wet. Put the sweet skewers right into a glass with sugar.

Tip:

Be sure to make a good mixture for the buffet. There should be something there for all tastes: vegetarian, with meat, sweet, and zingy. If the skewers are too little for some people, they can also use the glasses for a more ample buffet.

The skewers will stay fresh and tasty for about two hours.

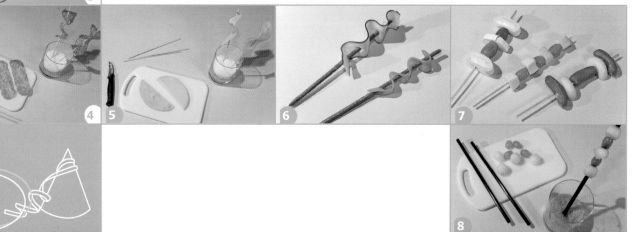

Text and photos by author unless otherwise noted
Copyright © 2010 Elisabeth Bangert
This book was translated from the German by Dr. Edward Force from the title *Garnieren & Verzieren* by Sammüller Kretiv GmbH

Library of Congress Control Number: 2010940049

Designed by IR
Type set in Advert/Zurich BT

ISBN: 978-0-7643-3645-4

Printed in China

Schiffer Books are available at special discounts for bulk purchases for sales promotions or premiums. Special editions, including personalized covers, corporate imprints, and excerpts can be created in large quantities for special needs. For more information contact the publisher:

Published by Schiffer Publishing Ltd.
4880 Lower Valley Road
Atglen, PA 19310
Phone: (610) 593-1777; Fax: (610) 593-2002
E-mail: Info@schifferbooks.com

For the largest selection of fine reference books on this and related subjects, please visit our web site at
www.schifferbooks.com
We are always looking for people to write books on new and related subjects. If you have an idea for a book please contact us at the above address.

This book may be purchased from the publisher.
Include $5.00 for shipping.
Please try your bookstore first.
You may write for a free catalog.

In Europe, Schiffer books are distributed by
Bushwood Books
6 Marksbury Ave.
Kew Gardens
Surrey TW9 4JF England
Phone: 44 (0) 20 8392-8585; Fax: 44 (0) 20 8392-9876
E-mail: info@bushwoodbooks.co.uk
Website: www.bushwoodbooks.co.uk